LEARN MEDIA LITERACY SKILLS

HOW TO IDENTIFY
MEDIA BIAS

by Marne Ventura

BrightPoint Press

San Diego, CA

© 2025 BrightPoint Press
an imprint of ReferencePoint Press, Inc.
Printed in the United States

For more information, contact:
BrightPoint Press
PO Box 27779
San Diego, CA 92198
www.BrightPointPress.com

ALL RIGHTS RESERVED.
No part of this work covered by the copyright hereon may be reproduced or used in any form or by any means—graphic, electronic, or mechanical, including photocopying, recording, taping, web distribution, or information storage retrieval systems—without the written permission of the publisher.

LIBRARY OF CONGRESS CATALOGING-IN-PUBLICATION DATA

Name: Ventura, Marne, author.
Title: How to identify media bias / by Marne Ventura
Description: San Diego, CA: BrightPoint Press, 2025 | Series: Learn media literacy skills | Audience: Grade 7 to 9 | Includes bibliographical references and index.
Identifiers: ISBN: 9781678209704 (hardcover) | ISBN: 9781678209711 (eBook)
The complete Library of Congress record is available at www.loc.gov.

CONTENTS

AT A GLANCE	4
INTRODUCTION CAITLIN CLARK AND MEDIA BIAS	6
CHAPTER ONE WHAT IS MEDIA BIAS?	12
CHAPTER TWO SPOTTING MEDIA BIAS	28
CHAPTER THREE CONFIRMATION BIAS	42
CHAPTER FOUR FINDING RELIABLE INFORMATION	50
Glossary	58
Source Notes	59
For Further Research	60
Index	62
Image Credits	63
About the Author	64

AT A GLANCE

- Bias is when a source favors a point of view. Some biases are unfair.

- Media bias occurs when the opinions of reporters or media outlets affect how they cover the news.

- The least biased media outlets simply report facts.

- Some biases are widespread. Others vary by media outlet.

- The media is necessary for providing voters with information about policies and candidates.

- Media bias can make it more difficult for people to make informed decisions.

- People should evaluate sources for bias before trusting a source's information.

- Readers can evaluate photo choices, story placement, and use of loaded language to spot media bias.

- Confirmation bias is the tendency for people to accept information that confirms what they already believe.

- People should seek information from unbiased sources and sources with different opinions.

- People can combat confirmation bias by finding information that does not support their point of view.

INTRODUCTION

CAITLIN CLARK AND MEDIA BIAS

Star basketball player Caitlin Clark was surrounded by reporters. She had been selected to join a professional team. Reporters were excited to hear from her. Clark called on a reporter. But the reporter did not ask a question. He used the time to flirt with Clark.

Women across the country were not surprised. The media tends to take women's sports less seriously than

Caitlin Clark played college basketball for the University of Iowa. At the end of her senior year, she was chosen to play professionally for the Indiana Fever.

Caitlin Clark hopes to inspire more girls to play basketball.

men's sports. Female players are often harassed. Reporters comment on the players' looks. They talk about the athletes' personalities. They do not focus on their talent. Women's sports are also given less attention. A study was done in 2022. It found that only 15 percent of sports media coverage focused on women's sports. The rest was dedicated to men's sports.

But Clark believes women's sports deserve more. She is pleased that more people are recognizing women's basketball as a sport. "It's fun to watch," Clark says. "Everybody loves it. It can be on the highest of stages."[1]

Support for the sport is growing. Millions of people watch women's basketball. But more progress is needed. Female athletes are still seeking equal treatment by the media. It is one of the many ways in which media bias affects people today.

MEDIA BIAS

Media is part of people's everyday lives. Television is a type of media. So is social media. Online news is media too. These outlets give people information. But the information is not always true.

Media literacy is an important skill for everyday life.

Sometimes the media spreads false information. Other times it has a bias.

Media bias is when a source unfairly favors a point of view. Many news sources have a bias. Sources with bias may ignore certain stories. They may report opinions as if they are facts. They might use sources that support only one point of view.

Bias can lead people to make decisions without having the full story. But media literacy skills can help people spot bias. Media literacy is the ability to **evaluate** media. Media literate people don't automatically believe what they read, watch, or hear. They check their sources. They read news from more than one source. Being able to recognize bias helps people be responsible media consumers.

CHAPTER ONE

WHAT IS MEDIA BIAS?

A bias is a preference for or against something. People can be biased against anything. They can be biased against minor things. They may be biased against certain foods. This kind of bias is harmless. But some biases are dangerous. People can be biased against ideas. They may even be biased against people. Bias is

Children learn biases at an early age by watching the people around them.

sometimes unfair. Racism is an example of an unfair bias.

Most people have some form of bias. Many are unaware of their bias. This is called unconscious bias.

Media often has a bias. Media bias happens when a news outlet shows favoritism in the way it reports. It presents news from a certain point of view rather than just stating the facts. People who rely

Is Bias Always Bad?

Not all biases are bad. Most people are biased in favor of experts. A person looking for advice about good eating habits is more likely to trust a nutritionist than a movie star. This is a healthy bias. Biases become unhealthy when they are made without a good reason.

on media for accurate, or true, information might be misled by media bias.

BIAS IN NEWS

Some biases are widespread. Many experts argue that the United States' news media is biased against people of color. This is shown in how the media reports missing person cases. People of color go missing at a higher rate than white people. But the media more commonly reports on cases where white people are missing. This is an example of bias.

People of color are also treated negatively by the news. This is particularly true for Black people. The media often treats them as criminals. This is true even when Black people are the victims

Media bias is a growing problem in the United States.

of crimes. A survey was done in 2023. It asked Black people how they felt they were treated by the news. More than 60 percent said news about Black people was more negative than news about other races.

Other biases vary between media outlets. Some news outlets are biased toward a particular political party. The cable channel

Fox News favors the Republican Party. This party typically supports **conservative** social policies. This includes the right to own guns. The party also supports lower taxes.

The cable channel MSNBC favors the Democratic Party. This party supports **liberal** social policies. This includes civil rights. It also supports using tax money for social services.

Political bias can be seen in the way each media outlet reports news. In 2024, Democratic president Joe Biden's son Hunter Biden was found guilty of lying on a gun-purchase form. Both MSNBC and Fox reported on the story. MSNBC's story read, "The president's son was indicted on rarely prosecuted gun charges."[2] This phrasing suggested that Hunter Biden's treatment was harsher than usual. Fox News took a different angle on the story. Its headline read, "Social media erupts over Hunter Biden guilty verdict."[3] This suggested that many people think Hunter Biden deserves his conviction.

Some news outlets strive to remain unbiased. The Associated Press (AP) is one such outlet. The AP's headline read, "President Joe Biden's son, Hunter Biden, is convicted of all 3 felonies in federal gun trial."[4] It remained unbiased by simply stating the facts.

Bias can also determine what news outlets report. They are more likely to report negative news than positive news. This is called negativity bias. Negative stories

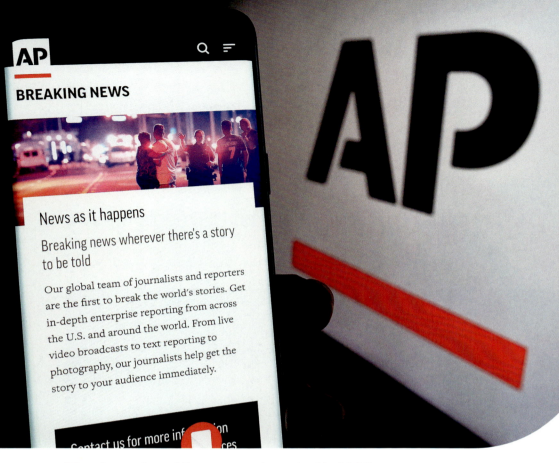

The Associated Press was founded in 1846.

are more likely to catch an audience's attention. This encourages media outlets to publish more negative stories. This trend has worsened in the past few decades. Dylan Matthews is a reporter. He says, "A recent study found that the 'proportion of headlines denoting anger, fear, disgust and sadness' grew markedly in the US between 2000 and 2019."[5]

News outlets are also biased toward certain parts of the world. US media often

The average person sees hundreds of ads every day.

gives more coverage to Western nations. A natural disaster in the United States or Europe might get more coverage than a disaster in Asia or Africa.

BIAS IN OTHER MEDIA

Bias does not appear in just the news. It is found in every form of media. Ads can be biased. Many ads show prejudice. Prejudice is a bias that is not based on fact. Ad bias can **stereotype** groups of people based on prejudice. Ads for cleaning products often show a woman working in the kitchen. Car ads often show men driving. These ads show bias about what types of tasks men and women do.

Ads are also biased against people of color. For many years, people of color were underrepresented in ads. This means they rarely appeared in ads. Ads were much more likely to feature white people. Many people in the United States still believe that ads have problems with this bias.

People of color are underrepresented in other forms of media too. Books are starting to feature more characters of color. But many of these characters are poorly written. They are stereotypes.

STAYING INFORMED

Michael Aliprandini and Simone Isadora Flynn wrote a research paper about media bias. It says,

> *Media bias is an important topic because of its potential effects on **society**, particularly when it comes*

to [people] making informed decisions about issues that affect [them] the most.[6]

Media bias makes it hard for people to get accurate information. This means people do not have the data they need to make informed decisions. The United States

The media can influence election results.

is a representative democracy. This means that the government is elected by the people. People vote to decide who should represent them. The media helps them decide who to vote for. News helps people learn about candidates' opinions. It helps people understand politicians' plans. Media also give voters information about how well their elected officials are representing them.

Citizens need to be well-informed in order to make educated voting choices. Media bias can make it difficult to be well-informed. This is particularly true for people who get information from a single source. The source may be biased toward one point of view. It might ignore information that has an opposing view. This can make it hard for people to make informed decisions.

When people become polarized, it can lead to political unrest and violence.

POLARIZATION

Media bias can harm society. It causes groups of people to become polarized. This means that people split into groups based on their opinions. It is healthy for people to have different opinions. But polarization can cause people to become **hostile** toward each other. Hostile people cannot function well together.

Luke Auburn is a communications specialist. He believes this problem is worsening. News stations are becoming more biased. The United States is also becoming more divided. Auburn says,

Some newspapers write intentionally misleading headlines to draw readers' attention.

"News stories about domestic politics and social issues are becoming increasingly polarized along **ideological** lines."[7]

Jiebo Luo teaches computer science. He agrees that media bias is a growing problem. He used a computer program to analyze 1.8 million articles from different news sources. The articles analyzed were published between 2014 and 2022. The computer program used the words in the headlines to identify bias. It found that sources were becoming more biased. Luo shared this information in a report. He says that the information might help people realize the importance of watching for media bias.

CHAPTER TWO

SPOTTING MEDIA BIAS

Today, many young people get their information from social media. This is not uncommon. But it is concerning. Anyone with internet access can post information online. A lot of the information online is untrue. Other information is biased. It is up to readers to make sure the information they read is trustworthy. Knowing how to spot media bias is an important skill.

Experts urge more schools to teach media literacy.

Though the internet can be used to spread false information, it can also be a great tool to fact-check information.

EVALUATING SOURCES

Evaluating sources is a good first step in making sure information is accurate. People should not believe everything they read. They should make sure the information is coming from a trustworthy source. They should also see if the source is politically biased.

AllSides can help. This website checks news outlets for bias. Readers can search news outlets on the AllSides website. AllSides then shows if the source is politically biased.

Other sources are harder to check for bias. Sometimes search engines can help. People can search for an author's name. They can read about the author's **credentials**. They can also research the source the information came from. Then they can read about it. They can see if experts believe the source is biased.

Biased sources are not necessarily inaccurate. They may have true information. They may even present it fairly. But readers should be on the lookout for bias. Knowing a source is biased can help readers determine whether they should seek out opposing opinions. Opposing opinions can help readers fully understand an issue.

Sometimes sources quote experts. Readers can research these people. They can review their credentials. They can decide if the quoted person has a bias. Then they can decide if the person is really an expert on the topic.

Often the expert has the proper credentials. Then the information is probably accurate. But sometimes the quoted person does not know much about the topic. Then the reader should not trust the source. The reader should instead find a different source that quotes reliable experts.

Credentials include degrees, experience in a field, and awards.

Sources will often cite where their information came from. They may cite studies. Others cite government officials. People can check these citations to make sure the information is true. They can also **verify** that the information was presented accurately.

Sometimes sources are not cited. Other times citations are vague. They may cite unnamed experts. This is a sign that readers should be suspect of the source's information.

Readers should also look at a media outlet's ownership or funding. Sources might be biased in favor of their owners or funders. This is called a conflict of interest. For example, the *Washington Post* is owned by Jeff Bezos. Bezos is the founder of the shopping website Amazon. This does not mean that the *Washington Post* is biased. But readers should be aware of the conflict of interest. They can look for signs of bias in articles about Bezos.

SIGNS OF BIAS

Loaded language is a sign of media bias. Loaded language refers to words and terms that cause people to feel a certain way about an issue. Loaded language is

Some articles have disclaimers that note possible conflicts of interest.

Politicians frequently use loaded language.

often used intentionally to sway a person's opinion. It is frequently used in the news

Some language is unbiased. The term *undocumented immigrant* is an example of unbiased language. But people can use loaded language to make people feel certain ways about this topic.

Some reporters use the term *illegal immigrant*. This term uses the word *illegal*. This is a negative word. It may be used to make people angry. This term suggests the reporter has a bias against undocumented immigrants. Other reporters use the term *asylum seeker*. This term uses the word *asylum*. This is a positive word. It might make people feel empathy. This term suggests the reporter is sympathetic toward this group.

Loaded Language in the News

People use a lot of loaded language when they talk about reproductive rights. People who support legal abortion call themselves *pro-choice*. People who oppose abortion call themselves *pro-life*. Both groups use positive language to describe themselves. This loaded language implies that the people against them are anti-choice or anti-life.

Images can greatly influence people's opinions.

People can be influenced by loaded language without realizing it. Readers with media literacy skills can spot loaded language. They look for the facts behind the story. They decide for themselves how to feel about issues.

Adjectives can be another sign of media bias. Adjectives are words that describe nouns. *Loud* and *crazy* are adjectives.

Adjectives tell readers how to interpret the news. A reporter might describe a politician's speech as *wild*. This shows bias. Another reporter might describe the same politician's speech as *passionate*. This also shows bias. An unbiased source would simply tell the reader what the politician said in the speech.

Comparing photos used for the same story is another way readers can spot bias. Outlets frequently use images that support their views. Opposing outlets will often use different images. An outlet with a bias against a politician might use an event photo taken before most of the audience arrived. This makes it look like attendance was low. A media outlet with a bias toward the politician might show a close-up photo

Some media outlets cover only one side of a story. This is called bias by omission.

of a small but crowded section. This makes it look like attendance was high.

Story placement can also show bias. Stories that support a media outlet's view are often featured at the top of the outlet's website. Stories that do not support a media outlet's views may be placed farther down the website. Other stories may not be covered at all.

CHAPTER THREE

CONFIRMATION BIAS

People tend to believe information that supports their previously-held views. They tend to dismiss information they disagree with. This is called confirmation bias. Kendra Cherry writes about psychology. She explains confirmation bias using an example:

> *Imagine that Mary believes that left-handed people are more creative than right-handed people.*

People are more likely to remember information they agree with than information that opposes their views.

Confirmation bias makes people more likely to befriend others with similar beliefs.

Whenever Mary encounters a left-handed, creative person, she will place greater importance on this "evidence" because it supports what she already believes.[8]

She goes on to explain that if Mary sees a creative right-handed person, she might think they are an unusual exception. This is an example of confirmation bias. This kind of thinking can limit a person's ability to make good decisions.

Experts believe that confirmation bias is human nature. It makes it easier to deal with information. This is especially important today. People get constant information about a wide range of issues. It is time-consuming to read everything. Confirmation bias makes it easier to process information. Pride also influences confirmation bias. People feel good when they find facts that they agree with.

Confirmation bias plays a role in deciding what news people read. Jonathan Kaufman is the director of the School of **Journalism** at Northeastern University. He says that many people say they want to read unbiased news. But their actions show otherwise. They instead go to news sources that reinforce their beliefs.

ALGORITHMS

Some news websites filter content for each reader. Social media websites do this too. The websites filter stories and posts by following a set of instructions called an algorithm. Computer scientists

Social media sites such as TikTok, X, Instagram, and Facebook all use algorithms.

write these programs. Algorithms collect information about the user. A fan of a sports team will click on news about that team. The algorithm will then show more stories about the team. Algorithms can be helpful in these cases. Readers get news about what they are interested in. The same is true for students doing research. A person may visit sites with information about sharks. The algorithm will then show news about sharks in the user's feed.

Algorithms can be helpful. They show people things they like. But this can also be a problem. Algorithms create filter bubbles. A filter bubble occurs when algorithms present only information that agrees with a user's biases.

A user might click on a positive story about a presidential candidate. The user might click on negative reports about the opposing candidate. The algorithm will see this pattern. It will create a filter bubble for the user. The user will no longer get facts about both sides of issues. The person will instead see information that agrees with the user's point of view. This prevents the user from having all the facts. People who do not have all the facts cannot make fully informed decisions.

Filter bubbles can lead to echo chambers. This occurs when social media users share content with people who agree with their biases. This can lead to users becoming even more biased. It can also lead to users believing everything they read online. They do not check for sources. They trust information that may not be accurate.

False Information

False information is information that is inaccurate or misleading. There are two types of false information. Misinformation is false information that is spread unintentionally. Disinformation is false information that is spread on purpose.

CHAPTER FOUR

FINDING RELIABLE INFORMATION

It is important to find reliable information. Readers can do this by finding sources that release unbiased news. Unbiased news sticks to the facts. It does not use loaded language. It is not controlled by the interests of the company that owns the news outlet. The AP is a source that strives to be unbiased. Its thorough and fair reporting has earned the paper fifty-three Pulitzer Prizes. These are awards for outstanding

It's important to use reliable sources to stay informed about current events.

Librarians and teachers can help students find reliable information.

news reporting. A memo sent out to AP Staff says,

> *Whenever possible, we want to emphasize specifics rather than **generalizations** or labels. Let's say what we know to be true and what is false, based on our reporting.*[9]

It is not always possible to completely avoid bias. People just need to know how to spot it. This skill is more important than ever.

Bias does not mean that a source is unreliable. But it means that readers should do research about what they learn. People can fact-check what they read. They can look for media outlets that have different points of view. They can find information from a variety of reliable sources.

Readers who find signs of media bias can also examine the source itself. They can evaluate how the source's bias might have influenced them. Samar Haider is part of a team that is building a media bias detector. He says, "It's not just about detecting bias but understanding how these subtle cues can influence the reader's perception."[10]

The Media Market

Five media companies control most of the media in the United States. The owners of these companies are wealthy. They donate money to presidential candidates. News stories about these candidates often show a positive bias. The outlets may have a negative bias against the opposing candidates.

AVOIDING CONFIRMATION BIAS

Everyone experiences confirmation bias. It is human nature. But being aware of this bias can help people avoid it. People can intentionally seek out information that contradicts what they believe. A person in favor of electric cars might explore the opinions of those against electric cars. A person against lowering the voting age to 16 might explore the opinions of those in favor. This exercise might not change a person's opinion. But it will help them become better informed.

Exploring a variety of points of view can also help readers avoid filter bubbles. The algorithms that keep track of a user's search history will see that the user is interested in different opinions. It will deliver a wider variety of information. This prevents the user from seeing information supporting only one point of view. Larry Atkins teaches journalism. He says,

> *Ideally, each of us should reach beyond our own echo chambers and seek news from a variety of media outlets and perspectives. We should be wary of facts and information that we receive from biased sources, and we should verify that information through other reliable sources.*[11]

FACT-CHECK WEBSITES

- ☑ **AFP Fact Check**

- ☑ **FactCheck.org**

- ☑ **PolitiFact**

- ☑ **Snopes**

- ☑ *Washington Post Fact Checker*

People can use fact-checking websites to verify the information they see. These sources are sometimes biased. But looking at multiple fact-checking sites can help people find accurate information.

GLOSSARY

conservative
describing a viewpoint that favors established customs

credentials
accomplishments that prove someone has experience or knowledge

evaluate
to determine something's value, accuracy, or importance

generalizations
statements that use specific pieces of data to falsely claim that something is true all of the time

hostile
unfriendly

ideological
based on ideas or beliefs

liberal
describing a viewpoint that favors social change

stereotype
a popular belief that people have of a certain group

verify
to determine the accuracy or truth of something

SOURCE NOTES

INTRODUCTION: CAITLIN CLARK AND MEDIA BIAS

1. Quoted in "Video, Transcript: Iowa WBB Pregame 4-6-24," *HawkeyeNation.com*, April 6, 2024. www.hawkeyenation.com.

CHAPTER ONE: WHAT IS MEDIA BIAS?

2. Jordan Rubin, "Hunter Biden Found Guilty on All Three Counts in Gun Trial," *MSNBC*, June 11, 2024. www.msnbc.com.

3. Gabriel Hays, "Social Media Erupts over Hunter Biden Guilty Verdict," *Fox News*, June 11, 2024. www.foxnews.com.

4. Randall Chase et al., "President Joe Biden's Son Is Convicted of All 3 Felonies," *AP News*, June 11, 2024. http://apnews.com.

5. Dylan Matthews, "Why the News Is So Negative—and What We Can Do About It," *Vox*, March 22, 2023. www.vox.com.

6. Quoted in "Bias in the Media: Types of Media Bias," *Columbus State Library*, May 28, 2024. http://library.cscc.edu.

7. Luke Auburn, "Study of Headlines Shows Media Bias Is Growing," *University of Rochester*, July 13, 2023. www.rochester.edu.

CHAPTER THREE: CONFIRMATION BIAS

8. Kendra Cherry, "What Is Confirmation Bias?" *Verywell Mind*, May 19, 2024. www.verywellmind.com.

CHAPTER FOUR: FINDING RELIABLE INFORMATION

9. Quoted in Gavin Phillips, "Top 4 Unbiased Independent World News Sources," *MakeUseOf*, June 11, 2023. www.makeuseof.com.

10. Quoted in Nathi Magubane, "Duncan Watts and CSSLab's New Media Bias Detector," *Penn Today*, June 28, 2024. http://penntoday.upenn.edu.

11. Larry Atkins. *Skewed: A Critical Thinker's Guide to Media Bias*. Amherst, NY: Prometheus, 2016.

FOR FURTHER RESEARCH

BOOKS

Tammy Gagne. *How Social Media Impacts News*. San Diego, CA: BrightPoint Press, 2022.

Duchess Harris and Tammy Gagne. *Race and the Media in Modern America*. Minneapolis, MN: Abdo, 2021.

Heather C. Hudak. *How to Evaluate Sources of Information*. San Diego, CA: BrightPoint Press, 2025.

INTERNET SOURCES

"How to Detect Bias in News Media," *Lehman College*, June 25, 2024. http://libguides.lehman.edu.

"In Brief: News Media Bias," *News Literacy Project*, 2024. http://newslit.org.

"Interactive Media Bias Chart," *Ad Fontes Media*, 2024. http://adfontesmedia.com.

WEBSITES

AllSides
www.allsides.com

AllSides helps people identify media bias. It rates the media bias of more than 14,000 news outlets. Its website also has resources to help people learn to spot bias and misinformation.

PolitiFact
www.politifact.com

PolitiFact is an award-winning, nonpartisan fact-checking website. The organization evaluates the validity of viral claims. Its website allows users to search for specific claims and to browse claims by politician or topic.

Project Implicit Youth
http://implicit.harvard.edu/implicit/youth.html

Project Implicit Youth is a series of tests created by researchers at Harvard University. The tests allow users examine the biases they have against different groups of people.

INDEX

adjectives, 38–39
ads, 21–22
algorithms, 46–49, 56
Aliprandini, Michael, 22–23
AllSides, 31
Associated Press, the, 18, 50–53
Atkins, Larry, 56
Auburn, Luke, 26–27

Bezos, Jeff, 34–35
Biden, Hunter, 17–18
Biden, Joe, 17–18
Brittanica, 31

Cherry, Kendra, 42–45
Clark, Caitlin, 6–9
confirmation bias, 42–46, 55

Democratic Party, 17

echo chambers, 49, 56

fact-check websites, 57
false information, 49
filter bubbles, 48–49, 55
Flynn, Simone Isadora, 22–23
Fox News, 16–18

Haider, Samar, 54

Kaufman, Jonathan, 46

loaded language, 35–38
Luo, Jiebo, 27

Matthews, Dylan, 19–20
MSNBC, 17

negativity bias, 18–20
news, 6–11, 14–21, 24–27, 31,
 34–41, 45–48, 50–56, 57

photo choices, 39, 41
polarization, 25–27
political bias, 16–18, 27, 31, 38–39

racism, 12–14, 15–16, 21–22
reporters, 6–8, 19, 36–37, 39
Republican Party, 17

sexism, 6–9, 21
social media, 10, 18, 28, 46, 49
story placement, 41

unconscious bias, 14

Washington Post, 34–35

IMAGE CREDITS

Cover: © Miguel Angel Partido Garcia/iStockphoto
5: © wellphoto/Shutterstock Images
7: © Erik Drost/Flickr
8: © Vladimir Vladimirov/iStockphoto
10: © Insta_Photos/Shutterstock Images
13: © Evgeny Atamanenko/Shutterstock Images
16: © Baza Production/Shutterstock Images
19: © T. Schneider/Shutterstock Images
20: © Sergii Figurnyi/Shutterstock Images
23: © Adam Kaz/iStockphoto
25: © Lev Radin/Shutterstock Images
26: © Thinglass/iStockphoto
29: © Drazen Zigic/Shutterstock Images
30: © fizkes/Shutterstock Images
33: © Michael Jung/Shutterstock Images
35: © Evan El-Amin/Shutterstock Images
38: © chameleonseye/iStockphoto
40: © Gorodenkoff/Shutterstock Images
43: © ArthurHidden/iStockphoto
44: © Odua Images/Shutterstock Images
47: © Viktollio/Shutterstock Images
51: © damircudic/iStockphoto
52: © Monkey Business Images/iStockphoto
57: © CarryLove/Shutterstock Images

ABOUT THE AUTHOR

Marne Ventura is the author of more than 150 books for young people. A former elementary school teacher, she holds a master's degree in reading and language development from the University of California. Ventura's nonfiction titles cover a wide range of topics, including media literacy, STEM, arts and crafts, food and cooking, biographies, health, history, and survival. Ventura and her family live in California.